The Space Telescope

Christopher Lampton

THE SPACE TELESCOPE

Franklin Watts   New York   London   1987   Toronto   Sydney   A First Book

Photographs courtesy of:
Space Telescope Science Institute: pp. 10, 34, 38, 42;
The Bettmann Archive: p. 17;
American Museum of Natural History:
pp. 18 (#320236), 26 (#328043), 27 (#328716);
Franklin Watts, Inc.: p. 21;
NASA/Goddard Space Flight Center: pp. 36, 45, 48, 62;
NASA: pp. 25, 60;
Palomar Observatory, California Institute of Technology: p. 54.

Library of Congress Cataloging-in-Publication Data

Lampton, Christopher.
The space telescope.

(A First book)
Bibliography: p.
Includes index.
Summary: Describes the history, goals, and functions
of the Hubble Space Telescope.
1. Hubble Space Telescope—Juvenile literature.
[1. Hubble Space Telescope]   I. Title.
QB500.268.L36 1987   521'.29   86-23351
ISBN 0-531-10221-1

Contents

The Space Telescope

The way we look at the universe around us is about to change.

Everyone has seen photographs of the stars and planets. These photographs, taken by scientists called astronomers using instruments called telescopes, show us important things about the universe beyond our planet Earth.

They show us that the Earth, on which we are now standing, is only one of nine planets spinning in nearly circular orbits around a star we call the Sun.

They show us that the Sun is only one of 400 billion stars in a bright swirl of stars called the Milky Way galaxy.

They show us that the Milky Way is only one of the billions of galaxies that make up the universe.

That's a lot to learn from photographs. But, as the saying goes, a picture is worth a thousand words. If that is true, then the millions of pictures that astronomers have taken of the sky must be worth a lot of words!

Yet we will soon have a new way of taking pictures of the stars that will let us see things we have never seen before.

In 1988, if all goes on schedule, a space shuttle will carry a large telescope into orbit around the Earth, where it will

An artist's conception of the
Hubble Space Telescope in orbit

begin taking pictures of the sky. It will then transmit those pictures back to Earth as television images.

No large telescope has ever taken pictures from such a great height. Unlike telescopes on the surface of the Earth, this Space Telescope will not be bothered by clouds or by the glare of automobile headlights or by dust and turbulence in the air. It will give us the clearest picture of the universe that any human being has ever seen.

With this new telescope, we will peer into the hearts of distant galaxies. We will look back in time, to catch a glimpse of our universe shortly after it was born. We may even see planets in orbit around other stars.

This new telescope is called the Hubble Space Telescope, or HST, for short. It is named after Edwin Hubble, one of the great astronomers of the twentieth century, who changed the way we look at our universe in much the same way as the telescope named after him will again change it.

Astronomers are very excited about the Hubble Space Telescope.

In this book, you will learn what makes the Space Telescope different from all other telescopes.

We will describe how the Space Telescope works.

We will tell you what astronomers expect to see when the Space Telescope turns its giant "eye" on the universe.

And we will talk about why the greatest discoveries to be made by the Space Telescope will be the ones that nobody is expecting.

Most importantly, we will tell you why the science of astronomy may go through a revolution—a period of great change—and why we will never be able to look at the universe in quite the same way again.

1

The Space Telescope is one of the most powerful tools ever created for examining the universe around us. But it is not the first such tool. In fact, it is only one in a long line of instruments that scientists have used in that ancient human pastime—staring at the sky.

Breathes there a human being with soul so dead that he or she has never stood outside on a dark night and gazed in awe at the stars?

The night sky is one of the most beautiful sights in the world, and it is available to everyone. Although the Space Telescope will open new vistas never before seen by human eyes, each and every one of us can study the stars simply by stepping outside.

However, there are scientists who make a profession of studying the stars, and who actually get paid for doing what many of us would do for free: stargazing. The scientific study of the stars is called astronomy. Astronomy is one of the oldest sciences. In fact, it may be the oldest science of all.

Long before people started writing history, they looked at the stars. Surely they must have wondered what these strange lights in the sky actually were. Perhaps they guessed that the stars were lanterns hanging from a great black canopy far overhead. Or that the Earth was surrounded by a dark sphere with holes punched in it, letting in bright light from somewhere outside.

These ancient astronomers also noticed that the movement of the stars through the skies had an important bearing on their own lives.

During the course of the year, different patterns of stars are prominent in the evening sky. Thus, the heavens are a kind of giant clock or calendar.

When certain patterns of stars appeared in the night sky, the early astronomers knew that warm weather would soon be arriving, and that it was time for farmers to plant seed. When other patterns appeared, cold weather was just around the corner, and it was time to harvest the crops. Other patterns might indicate that the yearly floods were about to occur, or that it was time for holiday festivals.

Because these patterns of stars, called constellations, were so important, they were given names, to make them easier to remember and identify. Usually they were named after animals, such as Cancer the crab and the Great Bear, or after mythological figures, such as Orion the hunter. In most cases, there was little physical resemblance between the constellation and the thing for which it was named, except by the wildest stretch of the imagination.

It was also important to measure the motion of these stars and constellations through the heavens. The more accurately the motion of the stars could be measured, the more accurately the changing of the seasons could be predicted. Therefore, the ancient astronomers developed instruments to gauge the motion of the stars.

The most important of the astronomers' instruments, however, were the ones that they were born with: their eyes.

Even today, we can use these instruments to study the stars, just by walking outside on a clear night and looking up.

However, the ancient astronomers had an advanatage that most of us in the modern world do not share. The skies were clearer then. Now, the night skies are filled with smog and the glare of city lights. In ancient times, the skies were an inky black, and the stars glittered in them like diamonds. To find such a clear sky nowadays, you would have to travel far away from any big cities and shopping areas.

In a sense, we can think of the astronomers' eyes as the earliest instrument for gathering "information" from outer space, information that told them important things about these mysterious objects in the sky. By looking at the sky, the astronomers learned the motions of the moons and planets, and probably made educated (though sometimes incorrect) guesses about what these objects really were.

Information is nearly useless, though, without a way to record it, so that others might benefit from what you have learned. The earliest astronomers probably recorded the information in their heads, and passed it on to younger astronomers by word of mouth. Later astronomers would have recorded information on papyrus scrolls or clay tablets, and still later ones on paper.

This information from the stars comes to Earth in the form of light. Because stars are hot, they produce light, much as a fire or a light bulb produces light. This light crosses the empty spaces between the stars and Earth. When the light reaches the eyes of astronomers, they are able to see the stars, and learn things about them.

In addition to their eyes, the ancient astronomers sometimes used other instruments to gather information about the stars and planets.

Some scientific historians believe that the ancient monument Stonehenge, near Salisbury, England, is one such instrument, completed about 4,000 years ago. An ancient astronomer who stood in the center of this giant ring of stones would have been able to determine the time of year by watching the position at which the Sun rose and set.

You might be surprised to think of rocks as astronomical instruments, yet they allowed the ancient astronomers to learn much about the nature of the skies. They saw, for instance, that certain bright objects in the sky were not part of the constellations, but moved on their own separate paths. The Sun was one of these objects, as were the Moon and the planets Mercury, Venus, Mars, Jupiter, and Saturn. (There were other planets, but they were unknown because they were not visible using the instruments available to the ancient astronomers.) These were important observations. In a sense, they were the basis for much of the work done by astronomers even today.

As their methods were refined, the ancient astronomers were able to perform more and more impressive measurements with their crude instruments. Greek astronomers were even able to make fairly good measurements of the distance from the Earth to the Moon and the Sun, more than 2,000 years ago!

Yet their instruments were not precise enough to keep the ancient astronomers from making crucial mistakes. For instance, most early astronomers believed that the Sun, Moon, planets, and stars all revolved around the Earth.

In time, as the accuracy of their measurements increased, astronomers came to realize that this was not true. In the sixteenth century, the Polish astronomer Nicholas Copernicus declared that it was easier to calculate the posi-

*Stonehenge, an assemblage of huge stones erected
by a prehistoric people in southern England*

Stonehenge, an assemblage of huge stones erected by a prehistoric people in southern England

tions of the planets if he assumed that the Sun was at the center of the solar system—that is, that the Earth and planets revolved around the Sun.

Forty years later, the astronomer Tycho Brahe built the greatest astronomical observatory of his time. With money given to him by the king of Denmark, Brahe fashioned the finest stargazing instruments yet built, and made many important measurements of the motions of the stars. His observations, as interpreted by his young assistant Johannes Kepler, did much to support the idea that the Earth and planets revolved around the Sun, although this was still not a widely accepted notion.

As advanced as his instruments were for their time, Tycho was still gathering information from the stars in much the same way as the ancient astronomers had gathered it: through his eyes. And he was recording that information on paper. In truth, Tycho probably took "naked-eye astronomy" about as far as it could go. Most of what could be learned about the universe in this manner had now been learned. A new method of gathering information from the skies was needed.

Shortly after Tycho's death in 1601, such a method was found. That method was the telescope, an instrument that gave astronomers a new and better way to catch light rays from the stars.

The telescope was made possible by an earlier invention: the lens.

Polish astronomer Nicholas Copernicus,
the father of modern astronomy

When a ray of light passes through glass, it can bend. A lens is a piece of glass curved in such a way that it can bend many rays of light toward a single point. This is called focusing the light. When many rays of light are concentrated together in this manner, they become very bright. Furthermore, the light carries with it a very bright picture, or image, of the objects that produced or reflected the light. The lens takes that image and focuses it.

According to legend, the telescope was discovered (rather than "invented") around the year 1604 by an apprentice to the Dutch lens maker Hans Lippershey. This apprentice, a lazy sort of person, was apparently spending an afternoon playing with his master's lenses. He discovered, when he took two lenses and held one at arm's length and the other in front of his eye, that distant objects became magnified and seemed close by. The second lens took the image formed by the first lens and enlarged it for viewing.

Lippershey, when shown this discovery by his apprentice, placed the lenses inside a metal tube, one at each end. By looking through one end of the tube, he could then comfortably view faraway objects. Thus, he produced the first telescope. (Other Dutch lens makers have claimed to be the inventor of the telescope, but Lippershey is the most likely candidate for this honor.)

Astronomers were quick to recognize the importance of the telescope. The great Galileo Galilei, of Italy, was the first astronomer to build a telescope, in 1609. When he turned it

Galileo Galilei, Italian astronomer and physicist

—20—

toward the skies, he made startling discoveries. He saw tiny moons orbiting around the planet Jupiter, and spots on the surface of the Sun (Galileo damaged his eyes by turning his telescope on the Sun, so this experiment is not recommended for budding astronomers). He saw that the surface of the Moon was covered with strange markings, later identified as meteor craters, and that the strip of light called the Milky Way was actually made up of millions of stars. Other astronomers soon built telescopes of their own, and found a whole new way of looking at the universe.

Through the telescope, it became apparent that the planets Venus, Mars, Jupiter, and Saturn were worlds, similar to our own planet Earth. Copernicus had been correct, or nearly so. The Earth was a planet like the other planets, orbiting around the Sun.

In a way, the telescope is an extension of that most important of all astronomical instruments, the eye. It extends the abilities of the astronomer's eyes to see the universe.

The importance of the telescope, though, is not just that it makes faraway objects appear larger. In fact, the stars are so far away that they do not appear any larger at all when viewed through a telescope, just brighter.

The importance of the telescope is that it gathers more light than the human eye, and can concentrate that light in such a way that we can see objects that are too dim to be seen with the naked eye.

When we look at the sky on a clear, dark night, we see several thousand stars, more than we could possibly count. Yet the stars that we can see with our naked eyes are but the tiniest fraction of the stars in the universe. Most stars are so far away that by the time their light reaches the Earth it is too dim for our eyes to detect. But a telescope can catch this dim light and concentrate it so that an astronomer is able to see it. Thus, we can see stars and other distant objects through a telescope that we could never see with our eyes.

The invention of the camera, in the nineteenth century, also greatly improved our ability to see dim, faraway objects. If we attach a camera to a telescope and allow it to gather light from the stars over a period of hours, we can take pictures that are far more vivid than anything we could see with our eye to the telescope's lens. During such a "time exposure," the camera film can record more light than can the naked eye. When we look at astronomical photographs taken through such time exposures, we can see distant objects that our eyes could never have glimpsed, even looking through the lens of a telescope.

As better and better instruments were made, the telescope replaced the naked eye as the instrument by which astronomers gathered information from outer space. And when the camera was added to the astronomer's tool kit, it gradually became the main way in which that information was recorded.

The telescope and, later, the camera ushered in a new age of discovery. What sort of things did astronomers discover? Lots of things, including some that we take for granted today.

For instance, they discovered that the stars were not just lights hanging in the sky, but were distant suns like our own, though much farther away. This may seem obvious today, but it was surprising news to many people in Galileo's time.

By the 1920s, it was also obvious that many of the blurry, glowing objects in the sky were neither stars nor nearby clouds of gas, as some astronomers had suspected, but were giant swarms of stars, which we now call galaxies. Some of these "clouds" of stars were shaped like giant spirals. Others were glowing spheres, bulging disks, or shapeless masses.

Our own Sun belongs to one such galaxy. We can see part of this galaxy on clear nights as a wide but dim strip of light stretching across the sky. This strip, called the Milky Way, has been known since ancient times, but only after the invention of the telescope did astronomers realize that it was made up of many, many faraway stars.

In addition, astronomers discovered that there were planets circling the Sun that had never been seen before the invention of the telescope. In addition to the six planets (including the Earth) that have been known since ancient times, three more have been discovered with the aid of telescopes: Uranus, Neptune, and Pluto. The last of these, Pluto, was discovered in this century, in the year 1930. The Sun and its planets, along with other objects orbiting the Sun, are called the solar system.

To increase the amount of information they could gather from outer space, scientists have built bigger and better types of telescopes. The kind of telescope built by Lippershey, with two lenses, one at each end of a tube, is called a refracting telescope. Astronomers quickly discovered that bigger refracting telescopes, with larger lenses and longer tubes, could gather more light from the stars. This allowed them to see dimmer and more distant stars.

The Whirlpool Galaxy, M51, in the constellation Canes Venatici, and a smaller, irregular galaxy

Opposite: a replica of the first reflecting telescope, which the inventor Sir Isaac Newton presented to the Royal Society. Above: the 200-inch reflector at the Mount Palomar Observatory is a direct descendant of Newton's six-inch telescope.

Unfortunately, there was a limit to how large a refracting telescope could be built. Large lenses tended to sag—that is, they were pulled out of shape by their own weight. Such a lens would give a distorted view of stars and galaxies.

Fortunately, there is another type of telescope besides the refracting telescope. The second type is called the reflecting telescope.

Instead of using a lens to bring light to a focus, a reflecting telescope uses a mirror. The mirror, placed at one end of an open tube, reflects the light toward a small eyepiece lens that can be used to view the image carried by that light. (Often, a second, smaller mirror is used to guide the image toward the eyepiece.) By looking through a telescope or attaching a camera to it, we can see faint faraway objects in space.

Because the mirrors in reflecting telescopes can be supported so that they do not sag, we can build telescopes with mirrors that are larger than lenses. This allows us to collect more and more light from the stars. All of the largest astronomical telescopes in use today are reflecting telescopes. The largest fully operational telescope in the world today is the Hale Telescope on Mount Palomar in California. This telescope has a mirror that is 200 inches (5 meters) across!

Although plans have been made for reflecting telescopes with mirrors as large as 600 inches (15 meters) across, there may be a limit to how big a reflecting telescope we should build—at least, on the surface of the Earth. Although larger mirrors can capture more light from the stars, they also capture more stray rays of light and record more of the turbulent activity in the layers of air between earthbound observatories and the stars.

The planet Earth is surrounded by a shell of gases called the atmosphere. This atmosphere is important to life on Earth, because it contains the oxygen that we breathe and because it shelters us from harmful rays from the Sun and stars.

At the same time, the atmosphere is a problem for astronomers. The gases in the atmosphere cause the images from space to shift and change. This is why stars seem to twinkle in the sky, even on a clear night. The problem is even worse when stars are viewed through a telescope, which magnifies this twinkling. This makes photographs of the stars seem blurry.

The smog that has been belched into the atmosphere by factories and automobiles has not helped the situation. Neither has the glare of lights that surrounds large cities, and even small ones.

Does this mean that optical telescopes—that is, telescopes that use visible light to gather information from the stars—are no longer useful and that the age of astronomical discovery is at an end?

Not really! Visible light—the kind of light that we can see with our eyes—isn't the only way that astronomers can get information from outer space. There are also invisible rays from space that carry information to Earth.

In the 1930s it was discovered that some stars, as well as other objects in space, produce radio waves in addition to visible light. These radio waves can be detected with large radio antennas. Using such "radio telescopes," scientists have learned many things about stars and other things in space that they never could have learned using optical telescopes.

In addition to light and radio waves, astronomers also found that the stars were sending gamma rays and X rays toward Earth. These rays are very much like light, but must be detected by different kinds of instruments. (We cannot see these rays with our eyes or with optical telescopes.) Unfortunately for astronomers, these rays are also distorted by the air around the Earth, more than visible light is. These rays are absorbed by the Earth's atmosphere before they can come anywhere near the ground. Thus, when astronomers built gamma ray telescopes and X-ray telescopes, they were forced to use rockets to shoot them high above the Earth's atmosphere. In orbit far above the Earth's surface, these telescopes could then use radio signals to send back information to astronomers on the ground.

If we can send gamma ray and X-ray telescopes into orbit, why can't we do the same with optical telescopes? An orbiting optical telescope could usher in a brand-new age of astronomical discovery, using the same method of gathering information from the stars that the ancient astronomers used: visible light.

2

A telescope in space!

It would be the solution to many of the problems faced by optical astronomers—astronomers who depend on visible light to bring them information from the stars.

But do we have the ability to put an optical telescope in space? Optical telescopes are big, and they are delicate instruments. Even if we could get one into orbit, who would repair it if something went wrong?

The idea of a space telescope was first suggested in the 1920s, long before there was any way of actually getting such a telescope into space. The man who suggested it was the German scientist Hermann Oberth, who knew that someday we would have rockets capable of lifting an object as large as a telescope into orbit. Two decades later, Oberth's followers were responsible for the largest rockets ever constructed until that time—the German V-2 rockets, which were used by dictator Adolf Hitler to rain deadly bombs down on England.

Later, many of these same German rocket scientists became American citizens and were involved in the United States space program of the 1950s and 1960s. It was this space program and the powerful rockets developed for it that made the idea of launching a telescope into space seem possible. By the early 1970s many astronomers, especially Lyman Spitzer of Princeton University, argued that the United States should put a telescope into orbit. (Spitzer originally suggested the idea of a space telescope as far back as 1946.)

NASA (the National Aeronautics and Space Administration) agreed. It was NASA that ran the space program. NASA had launched thousands of satellites and capsules into orbit, some of them with astronauts on board. They had even sent astronauts all the way to the Moon.

Unfortunately, building and launching a space telescope would be very expensive and NASA was running out of money. They had just spent billions of dollars putting astronauts on the Moon, and the United States Congress was reluctant to give them more money for a project such as the Large Space Telescope, or LST, as it was then called. The American public was starting to lose interest in outer space, and felt that the money NASA was using to build rockets would be better spent directly improving the quality of life on Earth. There was also disagreement among astronomers as to the importance of the LST; some felt that the money would be better spent building telescopes on Earth or on less ambitious space projects. NASA almost put the idea of the Space Telescope on the shelf.

In part, the LST was saved by the shuttle—the space shuttle. The space shuttles were to be a fleet of reusable spacecraft, which NASA planned to start flying in the late 1970s. (Earlier rockets, such as the ones that flew astronauts to the Moon, were used only once and then discarded.) The shuttles would be cheaper to fly than the big rockets NASA had used in the 1960s and early 1970s. The shuttle was the perfect vehicle for launching the LST.

Also, astronomers eventually came to an agreement about the importance of supporting the Space Telescope project and demonstrated this support to Congress, which gave NASA the money that they needed for the project.

The space shuttle also solved the problem of repairing the telescope if something went wrong, at least in theory. Shuttle astronauts could visit the telescope in orbit and make repairs on the spot, by pulling out the broken unit and replacing it with a new one.

Of course, these repairs would be expensive, but they would at least be possible. The telescope was to be so sturdily built that it wouldn't need many repairs.

Launch date for the telescope was to be some time in 1983. This date was eventually postponed because of problems in building the space shuttle—and the telescope itself—and again because of the explosion of the shuttle *Challenger*.

There were plenty of problems involved in designing the space telescope! For instance, how do you aim a telescope in outer space? On Earth, large telescopes are securely anchored to heavy mountings, which hold them in place while they are aimed by complicated machinery. Once a telescope has been aimed at the object in space that the astronomer wishes to photograph, the telescope mounting turns slowly and smoothly to compensate for the Earth's rotation so that the telescope can remain fixed on the object while the picture is taken.

In outer space, on the other hand, there is nothing to which the telescope can be anchored. Even if the telescope

Artist's conception shows NASA astronauts
servicing the Hubble Space Telescope in space.

can be pointed at an object to be photographed, how can it be made to stand still while the photograph is taken? (Some photographs, as we will see later, might take several hours to make.)

Even very small movements will be enough to blur a photograph. Therefore the telescope will need to remain very still while observations are being made.

Furthermore, because the Space Telescope would be looking at objects farther away than any ground telescope has ever looked, it would need to be aimed very precisely, just to find these very dim objects at all. Aiming a telescope this precisely is like "hitting a dime in New York with a laser 200 miles [320 kilometers] away in Washington," according to Edward Weiler, a scientist with the Space Telescope project.

The solution to this problem is a powerful system called the fine guidance sensors. When an astronomer wants to point the Space Telescope at a particular area of the sky, the fine guidance sensor system will look for a pair of stars, called guide stars, that it has been told will be in that part of the sky. Once it finds these stars, it will "lock on" to them. This doesn't mean that a sensor will actually touch the stars; they are much too far away for that. But it will use the images of these stars to determine if the Space Telescope is drifting away from its proper position. If it is, then the sensors will use special gyroscopic wheels to tilt the telescope back into position. The Space Telescope will be steadier than any telescope ever built!

But now we run into even more problems! The fine guidance sensors will need a computerized "catalog" that contains the positions of more than 20 million guide stars, so that there will be at least two guide stars available in every

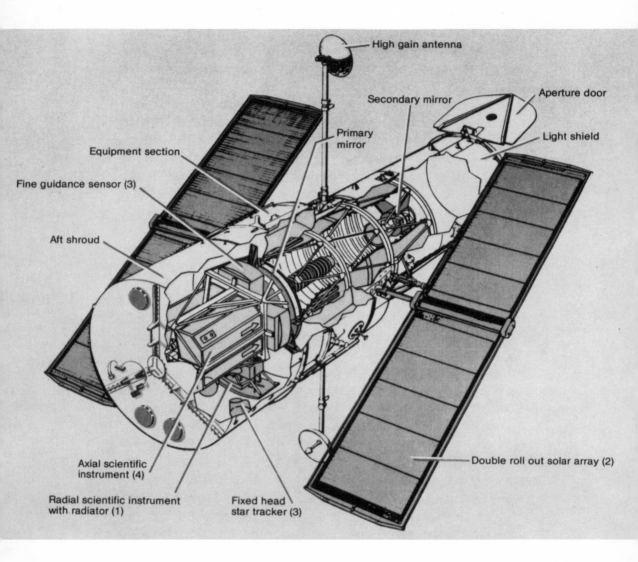

High gain antenna

Secondary mirror

Aperture door

Primary mirror

Light shield

Equipment section

Fine guidance sensor (3)

Aft shroud

Axial scientific instrument (4)

Radial scientific instrument with radiator (1)

Fixed head star tracker (3)

Double roll out solar array (2)

Cutaway section of the Space Telescope, showing the arrangement of mirrors and guidance instruments tiny sector of space that the telescope might be called on to photograph.

Unfortunately, no such catalog exists. Scientists involved with the Space Telescope have been putting a catalog together for several years, but it probably won't be complete in time for the launching of the telescope. A partial catalog will have to do. When the telescope is to be turned toward a particular portion of the sky, the part of the catalog dealing with that portion of the sky will be completed and radioed to the telescope's computers.

The scientists were also faced with nontechnical problems. For instance: who would be in charge of the telescope once it was launched? The obvious answer is NASA, because they are the ones who provided for the construction and launching of the telescope. But to manage the huge amount of astronomy research to be performed using the Hubble Space Telescope, NASA created a new organization, just to run the telescope. This new organization, called the Space Telescope Science Institute, was founded in 1981. It is located on the grounds of Johns Hopkins University in Baltimore, Maryland, about 40 miles (64 kilometers) from NASA headquarters. Its first director is astronomer Riccardo Giacconi, who has had much experience with astronomical satellites.

One of the Institute's jobs is to participate in deciding who gets to use the telescope. That will be a tough job. The Institute guesses that only one out of every five astronomers who wants to use the telescope will actually get to use it. Deciding which astronomers get to use it won't be easy. And the decisions will have to be made months in advance, to allow for the proper preparations to be made. Each astronomer, or team of astronomers, will submit a proposal

The Space Telescope Science Institute, located at Johns Hopkins University in Baltimore, Maryland

describing what they want to study with the telescope, and why.

Sometimes unexpected things happen, such as exploding stars or the sighting of a new comet. Astronomers cannot know in advance when these things will happen, and the Space Telescope could be very valuable in observing them (though it is unlikely that these events will be discovered initially by the HST).

To take care of these unexpected viewing opportunities, NASA and the Space Telescope Institute will allow director Giacconi to reserve 10 percent of the telescope's time to be used for things that he believes to be important. If he decides that the telescope should be turned on some newly discovered object in space which no one had anticipated, he can use this time for viewing that object.

When it is first launched, however, most of the Space Telescope's time will be taken up by the same engineers and scientists who built it. They will put it through a series of tests to make sure that it is performing as it is expected to.

In fact, for the first six months after it is launched, these scientists will be the only ones to use the Space Telescope. For the next six months, a full 50 percent of the telescope's time will be taken up with astronomy research by the project and instrument designers. Eventually, 80 percent of the telescope's time will be devoted to astronomical observation by astronomers from all over the world, with 20 percent of the telescope's time for testing the equipment.

The building of the telescope was completed by the mid-1980s. In the next chapter, we'll look at the telescope itself and see just what this wonder of technology is capable of doing.

3

The Space Telescope contains five different scientific instruments, in addition to the fine guidance sensor system. These instruments are controlled by scientists and engineers on the ground. Once these instruments have recorded their information, they radio that information back to Earth, where the scientists can study it.

These instruments are attached to the telescope itself. The Space Telescope is a reflecting telescope, with a mirror 94 inches (2.4 meters) across. This is not particularly big compared to some of the largest earthbound telescopes, but it isn't small. By comparison, the telescopes that amateur astronomers keep in their homes rarely have mirrors larger than 8 inches (20 centimeters).

The telescope, along with its instruments, weighs about 25,000 pounds (11,000 kilograms) on Earth. That sounds pretty heavy, but in orbit it will have no weight at all, because it is freely falling through space. This is the same reason that you feel lighter in an elevator that is just beginning to descend than when standing on solid ground, except that the Space Telescope will be continually falling in a circular motion around the Earth. (You can find a good book on

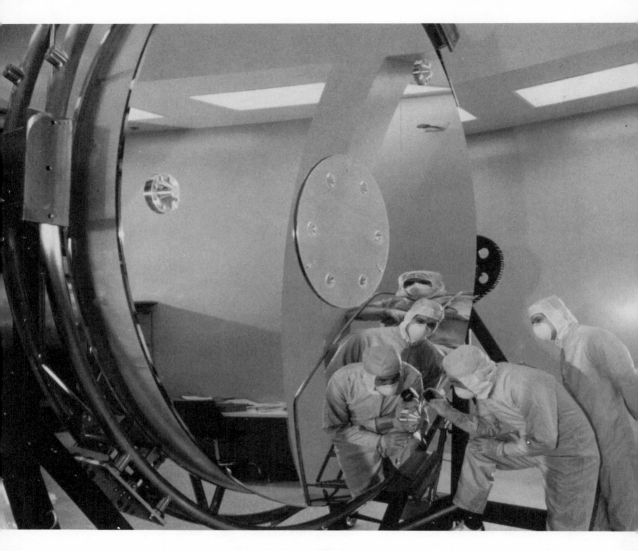

*The Space Telescope's large primary mirror,
which will capture images from deep space*

satellites that will explain this idea in more detail, if you are interested.)

It will orbit at a height of 375 miles (600 kilometers) above the Earth. As satellites go, this isn't a terribly high orbit. Over the years, its height will decrease because it will rub up against the outer fringes of the Earth's atmosphere. The space shuttle will have to revisit the telescope occasionally to lift it back to a higher orbit, else it would fall toward the Earth and burn up in the atmosphere, which would certainly be a waste of good equipment.

The telescope and instruments are powered by the Sun itself. Two winglike panels on each side of the barrel-like telescope are covered with solar cells. When sunlight strikes these panels, it is converted into electricity, which will recharge the six large batteries that will accompany the telescope into space.

Each of these five instruments attached to the telescope will record a different type of information. Here is a list of the instruments, and a description of the types of information they will be used to study:

The Faint-Object Camera. The faint-object camera, which is really a supersensitive TV camera, will take photographs of distant stars and other objects too dim to be seen with ground-based telescopes. It can photograph stars as dim as the twenty-eighth magnitude.

What does that mean? Magnitudes are the way in which astronomers measure the brightness of stars and other objects in outer space. The brighter a star is, the lower its magnitude. A star with a magnitude of 1 would be very bright. A star with a higher magnitude number, such as 10, would be much dimmer.

The dimmest stars that you can see with your naked eyes—on a very clear night—have a magnitude of about 6. The dimmest stars that can be seen through telescopes on the ground have a magnitude of about 24.

The faint-object camera will not only help us to see objects in space that have never been seen before, but it will give us much clearer pictures of faint objects that have already been photographed by ground-based telescopes. Not all of these objects will be stars. They will also include comets, clouds of gas floating between the stars, distant galaxies, and even stranger things, which we will discuss in the next chapter. Because these objects are dim and far away, these photographs will require very long exposures. That is, the camera must remain open for as long as ten hours, absorbing the light collected by the telescopes.

At a cost of 70 million dollars, the faint-object camera is the most expensive single instrument on board the Space Telescope. It was built in Germany by the European Space Agency, an organization that is assisting NASA and the Space Telescope Science Institute with the Space Telescope project.

The Wide-Field and Planetary Camera. The wide-field and planetary camera can, as you might guess from its name, take pictures of wider areas of the sky than the faint-object camera. (Actually, the "wide field" that can be viewed by this camera is only about one-tenth as wide as the Moon.) It can also narrow its view and take very detailed photographs of nearby objects such as planets. Some of the most beautiful pictures taken by the Space Telescope will be taken by this camera. In fact, this camera should be able to take pictures of

SPACE TELESCOPE

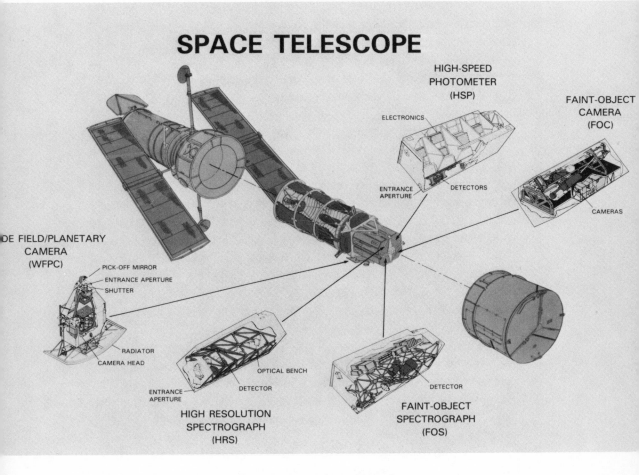

Artist's conception of the five
scientific instruments that will study images
captured by the Space Telescope

planets such as Jupiter that are as good as those taken by spacecraft that have actually flown all the way to the planet itself!

These pictures will not only be pretty, they will tell us important things about our solar system and nearby stars and even extremely distant galaxies.

The Faint-Object Spectrograph. The faint-object spectrograph will allow scientists to study the spectra of distant stars and other dim objects.

What is a spectrum (singular of "spectra")? It is the array of different-colored rays of light that a star, or other glowing object, produces. You may know that white light is actually made up of many different colors. In fact, pure white light is made up of all the different colors of the rainbow. You can see these colors by passing the light through a prism. The rainbow of colors produced by passing a light through a prism or a diffraction grating is called the spectrum of that light.

The faint-object spectrograph takes the light produced by the stars and other objects toward which it is pointed and spreads it out into a rainbow of colors, which are detected by an array of tiny sensors. What good does this do us? Scientists can use these spectra to find out what these distant objects are made of.

How is this possible? The light from a star contains all the colors of the rainbow, but certain colors are "stolen" from the light by clouds of gas and dust surrounding the star or drifting in space between the star and the telescope. When a scientist looks at the spectrum of a star, he or she sees black lines where certain colors should be. The positions in the rainbow where these lines appear tell the scientist what chemical elements are in the atmosphere surrounding the star, as well as about what the star is made of and how hot it is. The pattern of black lines is called the signature of the element.

Scientists have been using spectrographs to analyze stars for many years. The faint-object spectrograph is designed to analyze light from very dim stars.

The High-Resolution Spectrograph. Like the faint-object spectrograph, this instrument will analyze the light from glowing objects in space. However, the high-resolution spectrograph will concentrate on a special kind of light called ultraviolet light. We cannot see ultraviolet light with our eyes, and most of the ultraviolet light from stars is blocked by the Earth's atmosphere, so it cannot be studied by a spectrograph on the ground.

Other ultraviolet instruments have been launched into space on earlier satellites, but the high-resolution spectrograph can create sharper, more detailed spectra from the light of bright objects in space.

The High-Speed Photometer. A photometer (pho-TOM-e-ter) is an instrument for measuring the brightness of light. By pointing the high-speed photometer at a star, we can tell what the magnitude of that star is, and whether its brightness changes with time. This will help us to understand the nature of the star (or other bright object), and will help us to determine how far away it is.

The Space Telescope will be sending information back to Earth for at least ten years, and probably much longer. Of course, the lifetime of the telescope will be determined in

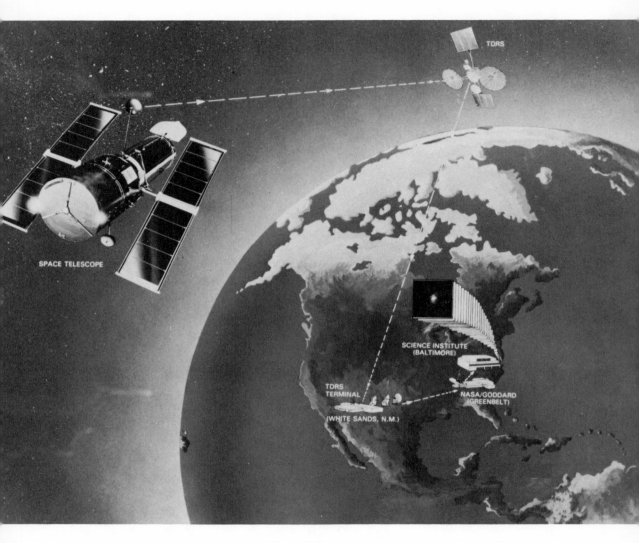

Artist's conception of the Space Telescope network, including the Tracking and Data Relay Satellite (TDRS), which will broadcast data back to Earth

part by the ability of the shuttle astronauts to replace old instruments with new ones when the old ones fail. Because much of the equipment in the telescope is designed for easy removal, it can be replaced in orbit if it fails. This will also allow scientists to design more advanced versions of these instruments to replace the current versions when they become outdated.

All of the pictures sent back to Earth will be saved as computer data, so that they can be analyzed again and again by astronomers. In this way, even astronomers who do not get a chance to "use" the telescope—that is, to decide what objects the telescope should be pointed at—will be able to study the photographs and information captured by the telescope.

The information sent back to Earth by the Space Telescope will become the greatest library of astronomical information—and one of the greatest libraries of scientific information—the world has ever known.

But what will scientists be looking for in this library? What sorts of things is the Space Telescope going to tell us about the universe beyond the Earth?

If we are lucky, the Space Telescope will give us the answers to some of the greatest questions in modern astronomy. It might tell us when and how our universe began—and even how it may end!

4

If we imagine that the universe is a large box full of stars, galaxies, and other amazing things, then the Hubble Space Telescope will allow us to see at least six times as many of the things inside that box as we have been able to see before!

Six times as many! That's a lot of things to look at! But, in truth, the Space Telescope will photograph no more than a tiny fraction of the objects in this vast area of space before it wears out from old age. Thus, astronomers will have to pick and choose, deciding what things inside the vast box of the universe are the most important things to point the Space Telescope at.

Of course, we are likely to make important discoveries no matter where in space we point the telescope, but there are certain questions that astronomers would like to answer, so it is important that they look into those parts of the universe where the answers to these questions may be lurking.

What are these questions? Here are a few of them:

How Are Stars and Planets Born? The Sun and other stars haven't been around forever. In fact, our Sun has only been around for 5 billion years, which makes it a lot younger than many stars. But where do stars come from? How are they born? And why does at least one star, our Sun, have planets revolving around it?

We already know some things about how a star is born, because we've seen it happening. Our telescopes have given us glimpses of clouds of gas and dust turning into stars, far away in space. We know less about how a planet is born, because we haven't seen it happening. In fact, we're not even sure if other stars even have planets, though we suspect that many do.

The Space Telescope will let us study the birth of stars in more detail. We can take a closer look at those distant clouds turning into stars. If we're lucky, we may even see entire solar systems forming.

We may even be able to see large planets in orbit around other stars, though these planets will be at the very limit of what the telescope can photograph. If we do see planets around other stars, it will tell us whether planets are a common phenomenon in our universe. It will also give us some clues to the conditions under which planets form.

If we don't see distant planets, on the other hand, it will not prove that such planets do not exist, but only that nearby stars do not have planets. Or that the planets are too small and dim for us to photograph.

How Was the Universe Born? This is a tougher question than the last one. In fact, it is such a tough question that you might wonder whether astronomers, with or without the Space Telescope, could ever answer it.

The truth is, astronomers already have a large part of the answer—or at least they think they do. If current theories are correct, the universe is between 15 and 20 billion years old. Originally, everything in the universe—galaxies, gas clouds, even the space between the stars itself—was crushed down into a tiny speck of matter so small that you wouldn't have been able to see it even if you had been there. We can't even imagine how dense this speck of matter must have been. All of the mattter in our universe, and all of the energy, was squeezed inside it.

Suddenly, this speck of matter exploded. This explosion is called the "big bang." As all of the matter in this speck was flung outward, it formed the universe as we know it today.

Is there any evidence that this big bang actually happened? Yes, there is. The most important piece of evidence was discovered in the 1920s by Edwin Hubble, the astronomer for whom the Space Telescope is named. Hubble was examining the spectra of distant galaxies that he and others had photographed through telescopes. (For more about spectra, see the description of the faint-object spectrograph in Chapter 3.)

Hubble noticed something strange. The spectra didn't look the way they were supposed to. All of the "signatures" of various elements (the black lines that these elements leave in the spectra) were in the wrong place. They had all been shifted toward the end of the spectrum where the color red appears.

What could have caused this "red shift"? Hubble assumed that it was caused by a phenomenon called the Doppler effect. Light coming from objects that are moving away from us very rapidly is "shifted" toward the red end of the spectrum.

Hubble and other scientists decided that this red shift meant that all the distant galaxies were moving away from us. The farther away the galaxies were, the faster they were moving away. It was as if all the galaxies in the universe

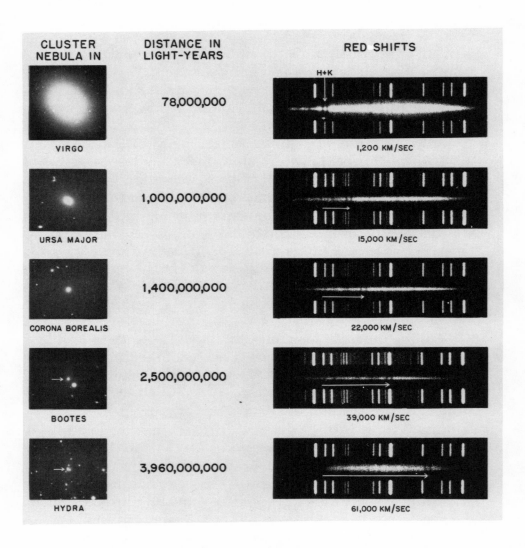

Relation between red shift and distance
for extragalactic nebulae. One light-year
equals 5.9 trillion miles.

were exploding outward from some unknown center. (Since all of the distant galaxies were moving away from the Earth, you might be tempted to guess that we are at the center of the explosion. You would be wrong. This is a kind of optical illusion; it would look the same from any place in the universe.)

Hubble's discovery was soon dubbed the "expanding universe." Cosmologists, astronomers who study the structure and history of the universe, theorized that this expansion was the result of a long-ago explosion, the big bang.

More recently, astronomers have discovered an "echo" left over from this big bang, in the form of low-energy radiation from everywhere around us in space called the cosmic background radiation. This is further evidence that the big bang really happened.

But astronomers still have a lot of questions about the origin of the universe. Exactly how old is the universe? How fast is it expanding? How long ago did galaxies form—and why? When did the stars and planets start forming? What was the Milky Way galaxy like in its first few billion years?

The Space Telescope may give us powerful clues to help answer these questions. It will let us view the spectra of very distant galaxies, so that we can see how quickly they are moving away from us (by examining their red shifts). But it will also let us look back into time.

How can that be? Well, we saw earlier that telescopes get their information from space in the form of rays of light. These light rays travel through space very quickly, but they cannot cross space in an instant. In fact, space is so vast that the light from the nearest stars takes several years to reach us. And the light from galaxies takes millions, even billions, of years to reach our telescopes.

This means that the information carried by this light is billions of years old. We are seeing these galaxies as they looked in the distant past. In this sense, a telescope is a kind of time machine.

The farther we can see in space, then, the farther we can see back in time. Will the Space Telescope allow us to see all the way back to the big bang? Not quite, but it will extend our vision billions of years into the past.

What will we see as we look back into the earlier years of the universe? No one can say for sure. However, when earth-bound telescopes look billions of years into the past, they sometimes show us objects called quasars. These are objects smaller than our solar system, but they produce a hundred to a thousand times more light and energy than an entire galaxy. Quasars are the brightest objects in the universe.

Although many quasars have been seen at great distances from the Earth, none have been found nearby. The most likely explanation is that quasars only existed in the distant past. We see them only when we study light from billions of years ago.

Quasars are a clue to what things were like in the early universe. Quasars may be fiery explosions taking place in the centers of galaxies, perhaps caused by black holes (which we will talk about in a moment). Will the Space Telescope see quasars? Certainly it will. But it will look farther into the past than earlier telescopes. It may show us how quasars are born, and give us clearer pictures of the quasars that have already been studied by ground-based telescopes. And we might discover even stranger objects that existed before quasars. Every such object that astronomers see will tell us more about the birth of our universe.

How Will the Universe End? You might think that this question could never be answered at all. Surprisingly it can be, if we can get enough information about the universe and what it is made of. The Space Telescope could help to supply this information.

The big bang caused the universe to fly apart. There is another force, however, that is working against the expansion of the universe—gravity.

Every object in the universe produces gravity. Gravity is the force that holds the planets in orbit around the Sun—and that keeps us from falling off the Earth and into space.

Even as the universe is flying apart, gravity is slowing down the expansion. If there is enough matter in the universe, then gravity will overcome the explosion that caused the universe to expand. If so, then eventually—many billions of years from now—the universe will stop expanding and start to collapse. It may even collapse into a tiny speck of energy matter like the one that existed before the big bang. And, if that happens, there may be another big bang, creating a whole new universe. And if that new universe collapses, there may be another big bang. And so forth.

In fact, there may have been other big bangs in the past, hundreds or thousands of them. Maybe these big bangs have been going on forever—and will keep going on forever into the future. The universe just collapses, explodes, and collapses again . . . and again and again and again. Astronomers refer to this as the oscillating universe theory.

On the other hand, if the force of the gravity created by the matter in the universe isn't as strong as the explosion that created the universe, then the universe will just keep on expanding forever. Alas, all of the stars will eventually burn out, and new stars will finally stop forming, and the universe will become a dark, cold, lifeless place. Not a pretty picture. The oscillating universe sounds a lot better, if only because new living beings may evolve in the new universe, while the gradually dying old universe would eventually become incapable of supporting life. (Of course, the human race will cease to exist under either scenario, assuming that the human race will survive for billions of years in anything resembling its present form. But these events are so far in the future that no one reading this book needs to make plans for either eventuality.)

Which will it be? Nobody knows. It depends on how much matter there is in the universe to produce gravity.

How much matter is there in the universe? That's not an easy question to answer. However, astronomers have tried to answer this question by looking at other galaxies, and at the stars and other objects in our galaxy. Then they estimate how much matter there is in the universe and calculate how much gravity all this matter produces.

So far, the answer is that there is not enough gravity to make the universe collapse. If so, the universe won't oscillate. But astronomers have reason to believe that there is a lot of matter in the universe that they cannot see. In fact, there may be ten, or even a hundred, times as much of this invisible matter as there is visible matter. Astronomers refer to this unseen matter, which may or may not exist, as the "missing mass."

Where is the missing mass hiding? Maybe it's in the hulks of old burned-out stars. Or in tiny, ghostlike particles called neutrinos that are so small that they can pass right through planets and stars without being noticed.

The truth is, nobody really knows. The Space Telescope will let astronomers search for this missing mass, peering around in this and other galaxies and in the spaces between galaxies to see if we can identify dark objects that may produce enough gravity to make the universe collapse.

And then we will know whether the universe will oscillate or burn out like a smoldering coal from a fire.

Are Black Holes Real? A black hole is the leftover remnant of a very large star that has exploded and collapsed. Much of the material of the very large star is squeezed down into a ball smaller than the planet Earth. This ball of matter is so tightly packed that it produces more gravity than any other object its size in the universe. Although the ball is still hot, and still glows like any hot star, the light it produces is trapped by its own gravity. Because the light cannot reach our eyes, the remnant of the burned-out star disappears from the universe. It becomes a "black hole."

At least, that's how the theory goes. No one has actually seen a black hole but astronomers think that they must exist. However, they do not have conclusive proof.

With the Space Telescope, we could look for black holes in space. But how can we look for something that is invisible? A black hole would have a powerful effect on anything near it in space. It would suck dust and gas out of clouds floating between the stars. It might even pull matter out of nearby stars.

This matter would form a swirling cloud spiraling around the black hole before it fell into the black hole and disappeared from sight. This cloud of matter would be very hot and would glow very brightly—and might be visible

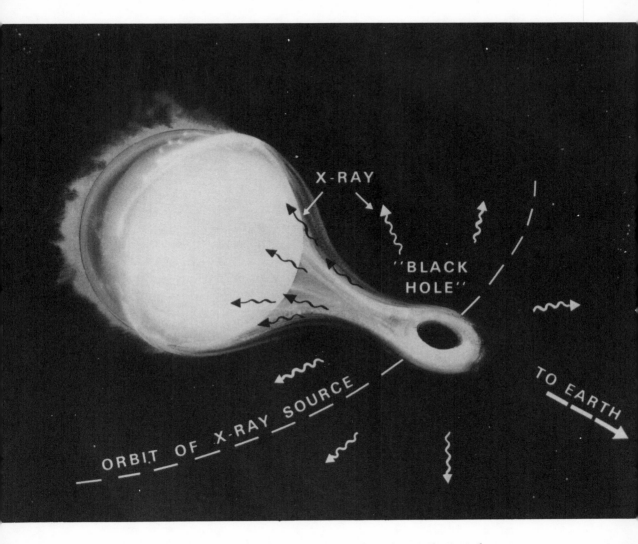

British scientists claim they have detected evidence of a visible star's gas clouds swirling around and disappearing into a black hole.

through a powerful telescope such as the Hubble Space Telescope.

Some astronomers think that black holes are the cause of quasars. Stars are packed very tightly at the center of a galaxy. A black hole at the center of a galaxy could swallow nearby stars and grow larger and larger, like a hungry monster, swallowing more and more stars as it grew. The cloud of matter around such a black hole would be extremely hot and bright, which would explain the intense brightness and energy of a quasar.

Eventually, this explosion might cool down. This is why quasars no longer exist near us. It is only when we look far away—back in time—that we see quasars, which are probably the cores of young galaxies.

However, astronomers have photographed nearby galaxies with explosions taking place at their centers. These galaxies, called Seyfert galaxies, are not as bright as quasars, but they may be quasars that have dimmed with time. Quasars may be an earlier form of Seyfert galaxies.

The Space Telescope could give us greatly improved pictures of these Seyfert galaxies, so that we can determine once and for all if they have black holes at their centers!

It is even possible that our own galaxy is a very old Seyfert galaxy, which was once a quasar! We cannot see the center of the Milky Way galaxy, because there are dark clouds of dust blocking our view. But some astronomers claim to have found evidence that there is a very massive object, maybe a giant black hole, on the other side of the dust clouds!

Perhaps these giant black holes are one of the hiding places of the so-called missing mass. Although the matter inside these black holes would be invisible, its gravity would still affect the rest of the universe.

The official patch of the Edwin Hubble
Space Telescope Project

These are just a few of the questions that astronomers will be asking as the Hubble Space Telescope sends back its first pictures of the universe.

Will the telescope provide the answers? Maybe. And if the past is any guide, the Space Telescope will also provide a lot of new questions to ask.

The more we know about our universe, the more we see what we have yet to learn. Every time a question is answered, two more questions take its place.

The greatest questions answered by the Space Telescope may well be the ones that nobody has ever asked. Thirty years ago, astronomers didn't even know about quasars or black holes or the missing mass. Ten years from now, we may be asking questions about objects that don't even have names today, because nobody yet knows that they exist.

If space is a box, then it must be one of those boxes of candy with toy surprises hidden inside. The Space Telescope will pluck out toy surprises that no one has even imagined are there, and lay them out where everyone can enjoy them.

Science would be very dull without unanswered questions. The Hubble Space Telescope may answer many of the questions that astronomers are asking today, but it should provide plenty of unanswered ones for astronomers to mull over in the decades and centuries to come!

For Further Reading

Berger, Melvin. *Bright Stars, Red Giants and White Dwarfs.* New York: Putnam, 1983.

Branley, Franklyn M. *Space Telescope.* New York: Thomas Y. Crowell, 1985.

Lampton, Christopher. *Black Holes and Other Secrets of the Universe.* New York: Franklin Watts, 1980.

Provenzo, Eugene F., Jr., and Asterie Baker Provenzo. *Rediscovering Astronomy.* La Jolla, CA.: Oak Tree, 1980.

Vogt, Gregory. *The Space Shuttle.* New York: Franklin Watts, 1983.

Index

About the Author

Christopher Lampton is the author of more than twenty-five books for Franklin Watts, including a number of popular First Book and Impact titles.

Mr. Lampton lives in Maryland, near Washington, D.C., and has a degree in radio and television broadcasting. In addition to his books in the area of science and technology, he has written books on computer languages and graphics and four science-fiction novels.